SQUADRONS!

No. 14

THE SUPERMARINE SPITFIRE MK. VIII

IN THE SOUTHWEST PACIFIC - THE BRITISH

Phil H. Listemann

ISBN: 978-2918590-92-7

Copyright

© 2016 Philedition - Phil Listemann
updated June 2019

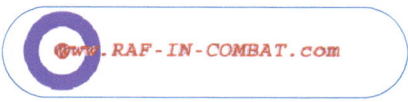

Colour profiles: Gaetan Marie/Bravo Bravo Aviation

All right reserved. No part of this book may be reproduced, stored in a retrieval system or transmitted in any form by any means, electronic, mechanical, photocopying, recording or otherwise, without prior permission of the author.

GLOSSARY OF TERMS

PERSONEL:
(AUS)/RAF: Australian serving in the RAF
(BEL)/RAF: Belgian serving in the RAF
(CAN)/RAF: Canadian serving in the RAF
(CZ)/RAF: Czechoslovak serving in the RAF
(NFL)/RAF: Newfoundlander serving in the RAF
(NL)/RAF: Dutch serving in the RAF
(NZ)/RAF: New Zealander serving in the RAF
(POL)/RAF: Pole serving in the RAF
(RHO)/RAF: Rhodesian serving in the RAF
(SA)/RAF: South African serving in the RAF
(US)/RAF - RCAF : American serving in the RAF or RCAF

RANKS
G/C : Group Captain
W/C : Wing Commander
S/L : Squadron Leader
F/L : Flight Lieutenant
F/O : Flying Officer
P/O : Pilot Officer
W/O : Warrant Officer
F/Sgt : Flight Sergeant
Sgt : Sergeant
Cpl : Corporal
LAC : Leading Aircraftman

OTHER
ATA: Air Transport Auxiliary
CO : Commander
DFC : Distinguished Flying Cross
DFM : Distinguished Flying Medal
DSO : Distinguished Service Order
Eva. : Evaded
ORB : Operational Record Book
OTU : Operational Training Unit
PoW : Prisoner of War
PAF: Polish Air Force
RAF : Royal Air Force
RAAF : Royal Australian Air Force
RCAF : Royal Canadian Air Force
RNZAF : Royal New Zealand Air Force
SAAF : South African Air Force
s/d: Shot down
Sqn : Squadron
† : Killed

CODENAMES - OFFENSIVE OPERATIONS - FIGHTER COMMAND

CIRCUS:
Bombers heavily escorted by fighters, the purpose being to bring enemy fighters into combat.

RAMROD:
Bombers escorted by fighters, the primary aim being to destroy a target.

RANGER:
Large formation freelance intrusion over enemy territory with aim of wearing down enemy figthers.

RHUBARD:
Freelance fighter sortie against targets of opportunity.

RODEO:
A fighter sweep without bombers.

SWEEP:
An offensive flight by fighters designed to draw up and clear the enemy from the sky.

The Spitfire Mk. VIII

Designed before the Mk. IX, but following it into service because its radical design changes would have meant production delays when time was of the essence, the Spitfire Mk. VIII was in fact a non-pressurised version of the Mk. VII designed for low altitude combat (see SQUADRONS! No. 6). At the outset it was the designated successor to the Mk. V, the replacement of which was planned from 1943 onwards. However, due to the slower than planned development, the first aircraft did not leave the assembly lines until November 1942. By this time the Mk. IX had recently entered service with Fighter Command and appeared to have a bright future. With the impending arrival of the first Griffon Spitfires, the RAF decided to retain the Mk. VIII for overseas theatres - the Mediterranean, Far East and the Pacific - where the replacement of the Spitfire Mk. V had become a necessity. The arrival of the Mk. IX forever sealed the fate of this version, often considered as being the more fully developed, and it was to always be overshadowed by the Mk. IX. The official number of Mk. VIIIs built is 1,658. Three-quarters were delivered with a Merlin 66 that provided maximum power at low altitude. The others were delivered in either the F. VIII configuration (273 built with the Merlin 63) or HF. VIII (160 with the Merlin 70). The last Mk. VIII was taken on charge in December 1944.

It was in the Mediterranean that the Mk. VIII first entered service at the end of spring 1943. However, it was in the Far East that it was most used as just under half of those built were sent there from the end of 1943. The Mk. VIII was intensively used, however, with more than 51,000 sorties flown - 27,000 in the Far East, 20,800 in the Mediterranean area, and the rest in the South West Pacific.

In the Pacific, 410 would come under the control of the RAAF including almost all of the HF. VIIIs (159 aircraft). Even though the Mk. VIII remained a high performance aircraft in 1945, the RAF had to rationalise its inventory at the end of the war and the Mk. IX and Mk. XVI were chosen over the Mk. VIII which was then withdrawn from service in the months following the end of the war against Japan. The Australians decided to go ahead with American types for the RAAF's main post-war fighter equipment. The Mk. VIII pilots only claimed approximately 150 kills (confirmed or probable), two-thirds of which were in the Mediterranean, a figure which appears small but which can be mostly explained by the fact that this version was used in regions where the air opposition was weak, or even non-existent, and just a handful were claimed in the Pacific region. Also, although this excellent fighter excelled in aerial combat, by the end of the war it was only used in ground support.

In Australia, the Spitfire Mk. VIII was given the denomination 'A58' in the RAAF nomenclature - **A58-300 to A58-550, A58-600 to A58-758**. Initially, the serials assigned to the HF version continued on from the last LF. VIII (A58-550) but the RAAF decided in early October 1944 to start numbering the HF from A58-600. Generally speaking, the Spitfire Mk. VIII in Australia was not widely used (about 150 of the 410 taken on charge never reached an operational unit). Of the two wings fully equipped with the Spitfire Mk. VIII, No. 1 (Fighter) Wing RAAF and No. 80 (Fighter) Wing RAAF, one was fully made up of RAF squadrons, Nos. 54, 548 and 549, and the other with RAAF squadrons, No. 79, 452 and 457. Each would have a widely differing war.

Spitfire Mk. VIII MT655 seen during a pre-delivery flight in April 1944. Powered by a Merlin 66, it was shipped out to Australia and became A58-520. It served briefly with No. 452 Sqn RAAF in December that year before falling victim to an accident and being converted to components.

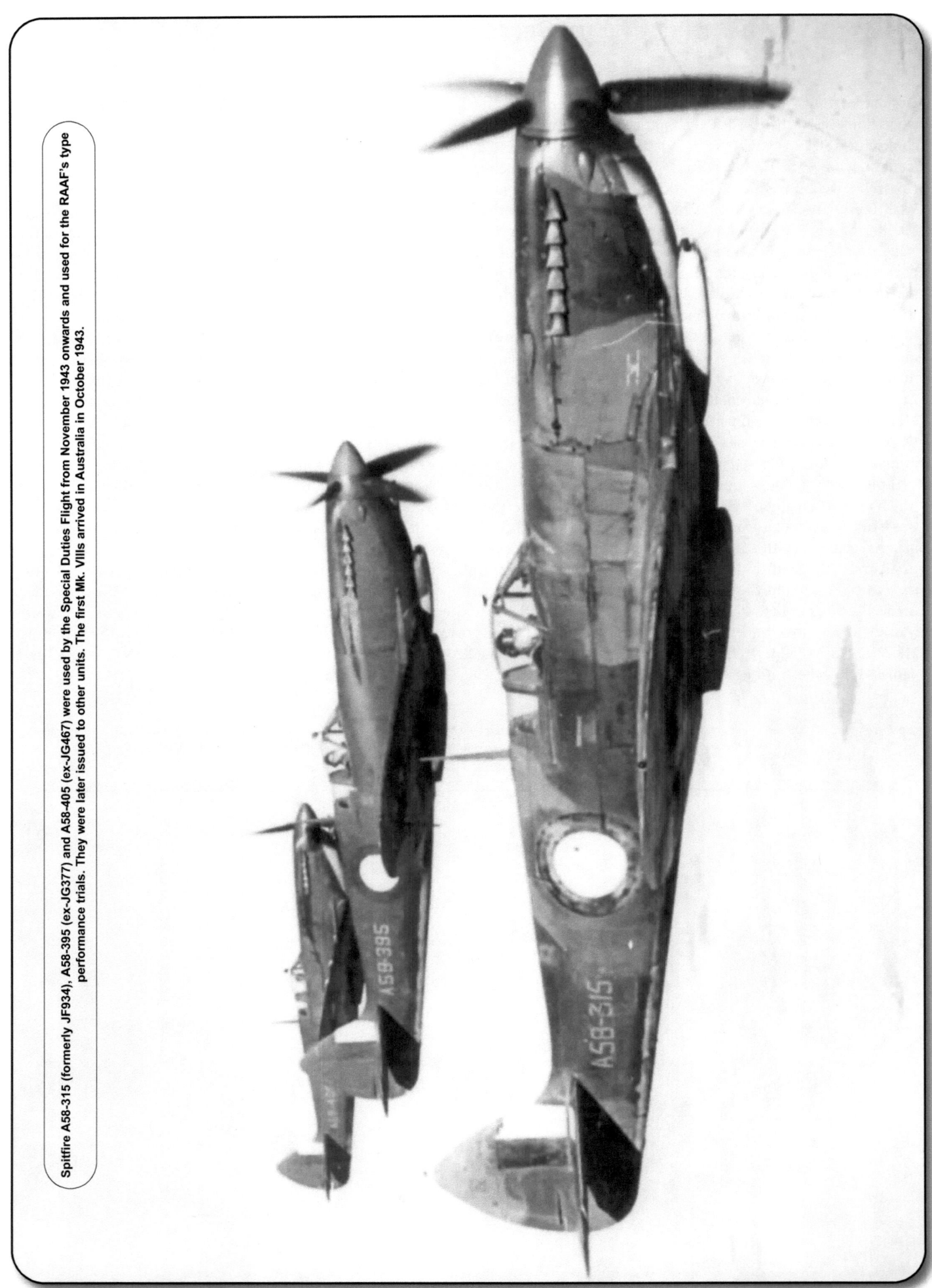

Spitfire A58-315 (formerly JF934), A58-395 (ex-JG377) and A58-405 (ex-JG467) were used by the Special Duties Flight from November 1943 onwards and used for the RAAF's type performance trials. They were later issued to other units. The first Mk. VIIIs arrived in Australia in October 1943.

The 1ST Wing, RAAF

Before going through each squadron history, it must be recalled that No. 1 Wing was first formed during W.W.I, as part of the Australian Flying Corps, then disbanded in 1919. It was reborn on 7 October 1942 as a fighter unit comprising two Australian (Nos. 452 & 457) and one British (No. 54) squadrons equipped with Supermarine Spitfires. The Wing provided air defence for Darwin and several other key Allied bases in northern Australia until the end of the war and had been rushed there in late spring 1942 to defend the area when a Japanese invasion was still a possibility. The three squadrons were taken from Fighter Command as requested by the Australian Government, which was seeking assistance, and Winston Churchill. This Wing is also named the 'Churchill Wing' because of his role in this decision.

Becoming operational early in 1943, No. 1 Wing intercepted several of the air raids conducted against northern Australia by the Imperial Japanese Army Air Force and Imperial Japanese Navy. Although the wing was hampered by mechanical problems with its Spitfires and suffered heavy losses in some engagements, it eventually downed a greater number of Japanese aircraft than it lost in combat. After the final Japanese air raid on northern Australia in November 1943, No. 1 Wing saw little action which led to its personnel suffering low morale. The Wing's two Australian squadrons were replaced with British units, Nos. 548 and 549 in July 1944 (but the groundcrew remained RAAF personnel), and subsequent proposals to move these squadrons to more active areas were not successful. This situation prevailed until the disbandment of the Wing in October 1945. From some points of view, it can be seen as a total waste of equipment and manpower when there was no serious threat of an invasion of Australia from the second half of 1944. This force could have been very useful in some areas, such as the Far East, as only about 250 sorties were flown by the British-manned squadrons in over eighteen months of operations. The morale and fighting spirit of all three units was severely impacted with 548 and 549 Squadrons being particularly affected as, unlike 54 Squadron, they had no combat record to fall back on. Even reduced to a single squadron, the anticipated political goal would have been achieved but with less impact. This situation can be explained only by a political decision from London to maintain a British presence in Australia because, from a military point of view, it was a total nonsense.

No. 1 Wing was led by two experienced pilots when it formed with the three British squadrons. Left, Group Captain, and officer commanding, Brian 'Blackjack' Walker. He was an Australian who had previously commanded 30 Sqn RAAF on Beaufighters and was awarded the DSO for his leadership. For WingCo Flying, the position was given to Wing Commander Roy 'Wilkie' Wilkinson (right), an RAF Battle of France veteran with a DFM & Bar and close to ten victories to his credit. He had previously led 174 and 1 Sqns in UK.

March 1944
October 1945

Victories - confirmed or probable claims: 1

First operational sortie:
21.04.44
Last operational sortie:
03.08.45

Number of sorties: 215
Total aircraft written-off: 10
Aircraft lost on operations: -
Aircraft lost in accidents: 10

Squadron code letters:
DL

Commanding Officers

S/L Robert B. Newton	RAF No. 88464	RAF	...	27.07.44
S/L Sidney Linnard	RAF No. 40179	RAF	27.07.44	01.07.45
S/L John B.H. Nicholas	RAF No. 39798	RAF	01.07.45	...

Squadron Usage

Number 54 Squadron is unique as it is the only RAF squadron to have been sent to the Pacific to reinforce the defence of Australia. It had previously fought under Fighter Command authority from the beginning of the war and had become one of the most successful fighter units. This had been one of the reasons why it was selected to be sent to Australia as part of the 'Churchill Wing' in the first half of 1942. With the two Australian squadrons, Nos. 452 and 457, 54 fought brilliantly over Darwin with its Mk. Vs claiming more than 25 enemy aircraft within a couple of weeks. By the end of 1943, as the first Mk. VIIIs were reaching Australia, Japanese activity had dropped off and 54, as with the other units of the Wing were now more engaged in routine activity than air combat.

1944 was a year of renewal for 54. First, a new CO took command. Squadron Leader Robert B. Newton had previously served in Europe and been awarded a DFC. In March, the squadron took charge of its first Mk. VIIIs almost by accident. Indeed, on 9 March, the two other squadrons of the Wing at that time, 452 and 457, had to leave the area at very short notice and 54 was left with the responsibility to assume a state of mobility in case of a move to reinforce them. Some of the Mk. Vs used by the squadron were therefore replaced by Mk. VIIIs used by the Australians but, as the pilots

> Sid Linnard was a pre-war fighter pilot with 80 Sqn flying Gladiators and began his wartime flying in Egypt against the Italians where he made his first claims. He later served as OC 274 Sqn and ended his tour in February 1942 with seven confirmed victories to his tally and a DFC.
> After a period of rest and instructing, he was posted to Australia to take over 54 Sqn for his second tour. He would lead 54 during most of the Spitfire VIII era.

Spitfire A58-370/DL-W under camouflage netting with its groundcrew and pilot in April 1945. Stored when it arrived in Australia, its RAF Desert camouflage was not changed at first. When 54 needed replacement aircraft early in 1945, when most of its VIIIs were sent back for overhaul, A58-370 was issued to the squadron in its desert scheme and large RAAF roundel. This was temporary and A58-370 was soon repainted. *(AHM of WA)*

would discover, the Mk. VIIIs were not used and replacement Mk. Vs were actually delivered. It was not until the end of March and the beginning of April that the transition took place with four Mk. VIIIs received on the 5th (the aircraft were handed over by 452 Squadron). The flow of new aircraft continued over the following days but operational requirements were still met by the Mk. Vs. However, some pilots were comfortable enough to carry out operational flights. On the 19th, Flying Officer P.G.F. Brown was tasked to ferry a Spitfire (A58-309) from Gorrie to Darwin. He took the aircraft from 14 ARD where it had been repaired after an accident while being flown by a pilot from 452 Squadron. Brown was not flying alone. He was accompanied by W/O Ross who was ferrying

Right side view of A58-370 in its desert camouflage of Dark Earth, Middle Stone and Azure Blue. The rudder seems to be a replacement. *(AHM of WA)*

Flight Lieutenants Gossland (centre) and Meakin (right) pose after they shot down a 'Dinah' on 20 July 1945. This would be the 54 Sqn's only claim while flying the Spitfire VIII. *(Andrew Thomas)*

another Spitfire (A58-330). At 9,000 feet, about forty miles south of Pine Creek, Brown advised Ross that his engine had cut. The pilot glided down searching for a place to crash-land. When at around 1,000 feet, and still unable to locate a suitable patch, Brown advised Ross that he was going to bail out, which he did at about 400-500 feet. The pilot opened his chute successfully while the Spitfire crashed into the ground and exploded. The unlucky Brown was not high enough to avoid the flames and went straight into them. Having opened his parachute too low, the speed was very high when he hit the ground and he broke his legs which prevented a rapid escape. His injuries and burns were too severe to survive and he died later that day. Having joined the squadron in November 1943 for a second tour, Brown was a young Londoner who had joined the RAF in 1941 and had fought with the 234 Squadron in England. On 21 April Flight Sergeants Portas (A58-330) and Nash (A58-304) scrambled at 0825 to intercept an unidentified aircraft but this was uneventful and both aircraft returned at 0915. The next day, another scramble in the middle of the afternoon was carried out, this time by four pilots, but the aircraft proved to be a Beaufort. Three days later, the squadron was called on to undertake convoy patrols with two aircraft relieved hourly from 0730 to 1300 and the Mk. VIIIs participated in eight. Finally, to close the air activity for April, on the last day of the month two operational exercises were carried out to secure data on the performance of the Mk. VIII. The exercises consisted of reconnaissance sorties of the Goulburn Islands at 25,000 feet, meaning a 380 mile round trip, and of Tindal at 30,000 feet, a 360 mile round trip. Each was completed in more than two hours flight time.

In May, the squadron achieved 200 hours on operations and twice that figure on training. The squadron was still flying both types with close to 100 sorties carried out as far as the Mk. VIII was concerned. This was possible because, from the 9th, a detachment was sent to Exmouth Gulf where patrols were flown until the end of the month. June, if we exclude the move to Livingstone, was quiet with about forty sorties carried out (mostly interceptions of friendly aircraft). Including training flights, 475 hours were flown. During the move however, which took place on the 8th, Flying Officer W.H. Doerr (RAAF) overshot on landing and damaged Spitfire A58-330. The aircraft was sent away for repairs, but, pending some unknown decision, no work was performed. Considering the number of unused Spitfires, it is understandable that it was scrapped the following April. The squadron lost another Spitfire in June, the pilot was unhurt, but the fate of A58-318, which made a heavy night landing on 14 June, was rapidly decided as it was judged damaged beyond economical repair and scrapped in July. Air activity in July remained constant with 483 hours flown but with less scrambles. The detachment sent to Drysdale was responsible for the destruction of a 'Dinah' on 20 July 1945, the victorious pilots being F/L D.M. Gossland and F/L V.F. Meakin. They took off on scramble when they sighted a 'Dinah' approaching Drysdale Strip at 27,000 feet. As they approached the Japanese aircraft from astern, they saw it dropping clusters of aerial fragmentation bombs which burst below and behind the two Spitfires. Gossland made his attack from a the stern left side and he saw his burst striking the left fuselage, the left wing and both engines. Then, the 'Dinah' sent into a steep dive and Meakin fires a burst which caused the right wing to break away; the 'Dinah' burst into flames and crashed into the sea five miles north of the Strip. The latter would enjoy his success for only a short time as he would be killed on 28 July when he hit a treetop, during a ground attack exercise, and blew up upon hitting the ground. The previous day, S/L Newton had relinquished his command to S/L Linnard DFC. In August, the number of sorties dropped to thirty. All of the scrambles were fruitless as all of the aircraft intercepted were friendly or an unidentified plot. The only other event was the wheels-up landing of A58-310 when it returned from a non-operational flight on 7 August. The pilot, F/Sgt Blair, escaped injury and the aircraft was repaired at the squadron only to be lost on 5 October during the flight test. The pilot, W/O P. Fox, was killed when the aircraft crashed into the sea for unknown reasons. The squadron ended its month when the CO led three other pilots on a sweep of Selaru Island. The target was a camp near Lingat village and the Spitfires were accompanied by four aircraft each from 548 and 549 Squadrons. The target was strafed and all aircraft returned to base after 2.5 hours in the air. The rest of the month was uneventful with only practice flights to keep the pilots occupied. In October, only three operational scrambles were flown, two on the 5th and the one on the 9th, and no more operational flights would be flown until the end of the year. Practice flights continued during this period and several accidents occurred. On 1 November, while practicing a GCI with three other Spitfires of the squadron (two used as the target, the other two as interceptors), W/O S.C.J. Laundy, who was flying one of the target aircraft, broke away from his number 1 because of a loss of power at the end of the exercise. Laundy attempted a forced landing on a beach but ditched in the sea instead. He was rescued, shocked but alive, and after a short stay in hospital would return to the squadron one week later.

In 1945, the squadron saw very little operational activity. In January, only six scrambles were recorded with the biggest day being the 16th when three Spitfires - flown by F/L Thompson (A58-476/DL-W), W/O F.R. Booker (A58-488/DL-T) and F/L Todd (A58-358/DL-M) - took off between 0940 and 0945 to finally identify a B-25 returning to base. In February, no operational flights were recorded with only two in March. One of these was a night scramble at 0430 in the early hours of the 5th for a B-24 returning to base (F/L Grierson-Jackson in A58-408/DL-T and F/Sgt Hicks in A58-327/DL-J). No scrambles were carried out in April and May but a Spitfire was lost on 30 April when F/L K.J. Bellamy crashed his A58-356 on the strip at Hughes at the end of a bomber co-operation exercise. The pilot was uninjured but the Spitfire was a total loss. On 3 June, three Spitfires of the squadron participated in a raid to destroy ground targets on Cape Chater aerodrome, Timor. They flew as top cover for RAAF Liberators. The pilots were F/L J.B.M. Nicholas (A58-370/DL-W), F/L M.W. Grierson-Jackson (A58-496/DL-D) and P/O F.R. Booker (A58-360/DL-R) but, owing to a faulty belly tank, Grierson-Jackson was forced to return to base. The operation was a complete success. On 17 June, as usual, many exercises were carried out with four Spitfires flying *Rhubarb* sorties in the morning but, sadly, in the afternoon, F/O F.F. Thomas lost his life while conducting an air test in A58-479 (he was previously involved in the loss on landing of A58-474 in March 1945). The engine failed on approach and the aircraft dived vertically into the ground. The rest of June was uneventful. On 1 July, S/L Linnard, who was returning to the UK, relinquished command to F/L J.B.H. Nicholas. Otherwise, July was a quiet month if we ignore the wreck of A58-462. Caught on 19 July by a gust of wind while taxiing after landing, the Spitfire weather-cocked, went into a ditch and ended up on its nose. It was never repaired as it was still being assessed when the end of the war was declared. The next day, an interception was made by two Spitfires (F/L Hack in A58-428/DL-B and P/O Laundy in A58-349/DL-F), who were diverted from a practice flight, but the aircraft again proved friendly. Another scramble took place on 3 August but the aircraft was a Mosquito (W/O B.A.G. Hicks in A58-480/DL-Y and F/Sgt Cudlip in A58-397). This scramble

Spitfire A58-352/DL-N was flown by W/O E. Rayner for the raid on Selaru Island on 5 September 1944. For this raid, all of the Spitfires carried a 90-gallon slipper tank as shown here. This Spitfire is also equipped with under-wing bomb racks which began to be appear towards the end of 1944.
(AHM of WA)

would be the last squadron operation of the war with the cessation of the hostilities with Japan coming a couple of days later. In all, 215 sorties were flown over eighteen months. The squadron was ordered to move south as its strength diminished rapidly. On 23 September, the squadron was officially based at Melbourne but had not been operational for a long time. It was officially disbanded on 31 October.

Claims - 54 Squadron (Confirmed and Probable)

Date	Pilot	SN	Origin	Type	Serial	Code	Nb	Cat.
20.07.44	F/L Derek M. **Gossland**	RAF No. 60823	RAF	Ki-46	**A58-312**		0.5	C
	F/L Frederick **Meakin**	RAF No. 1123140	RAF		**A58-390**	DL-M	0.5	C
		Total: 1.0						

Spitfire A58-318/DL-F lying on its belly after the landing gear collapsed after a heavy landing. The aircraft was not repaired.
(AHM of WA)

Summary of the aircraft lost by accident - 54 Squadron

Date	Pilot	S/N	Origin	Serial	Code	Fate
19.04.44	F/O Peter G.F. **Brown**	RAF No. 120926	RAF	**A58-309**		†
08.06.44	F/O William H. **Doerr**	Aus. 16417	RAAF	**A58-330**	DL-C	-
14.06.44	Sgt William G. **Hayward**	RAF No. 1316153	RAF	**A58-318**	DL-F	-
28.07.44	F/L Frederick **Meakin**	RAF No. 1123140	RAF	**A58-390**	DL-M	†
05.10.44	W/O Peter **Fox**	RAF No. 1119366	RAF	**A58-310**	DL-Y	†
01.11.44	W/O Sidney C.J. **Laundy**	RAF No. 1147350	RAF	**A58-302**		-
25.03.45	F/O Frederick F. **Thomas**	RAF No. 155264	RAF	**A58-474**	DL-E	-
30.04.45	F/L Kenneth J. **Bellamy**	RAF No. 150062	RAF	**A58-356**	DL-U	-
17.06.45	F/O Frederick F. **Thomas**	RAF No. 155264	RAF	**A58-479**	DL-H	†
19.07.45	P/O Francis R. **Booker**	RAF No. 197212	RAF	**A58-462**	DL-S	-
		Total: 10				

April 1944
August 1945

Victories - confirmed or probable claims: -

First operational sortie:
05.09.44
Last operational sortie:
03.06.45

Number of sorties: 18

Total aircraft written-off: 9

Aircraft lost on operations: -
Aircraft lost in accidents: 9

Squadron code letters:
TS

Commanding Officers

S/L William H.A. Wright (†)	RAF No. 70834	RAF	...	19.04.44
S/L Raymond A. Watts	RAF No. 65530	RAF	20.04.44	08.02.45
S/L Ernest D. Glaser	RAF No. 82178	RAF	09.02.45	09.10.45

Squadron Usage

Number 548 Squadron was officially formed on 15 December 1943, at Lawton, Queensland, Australia, but it was some time before personnel joined the new unit. The pilots, coming from the United Kingdom, only arrived in Brisbane on 1 January and joined later in the month, while the original CO, S/L W.H.A. Wright, a former 130 Squadron pilot, arrived at the squadron on the 2nd. The unit relocated to Strathpine but did not receive any aircraft until a Wirraway and a Tiger Moth were issued on 5 February. The first Spitfires, all LFs, did not arrive until 6 April. Deliveries did not get off to a good start as the first Spitfire to arrive (A58-396) overshot while landing at Strathpine on the 6th and had to be sent back to the Air Depot! The next day, three more Spitfires arrived safely, A58-392, A58-393 and A58-398. Bad luck continued, however, and on the 19th, a sad accident occurred during a practice flight. A section of three Spitfires of A Flight (F/O Hilton, F/L Price and Sgt A.V. Chandler) had taken off at 0845 and, after having orbited the strip, decided to bounce a Spitfire that had just taken off and was climbing down sun. The section closed to 250 yards at about 2,500 feet and broke away to the right. F/O Hilton then banked to the left to make sure that F/L Price and Sgt Chandler

Dave Glaser would become 548 Squadron's last CO. He led the unit from February 1945 until disbandment. He had previously served in England with 65 and 234 Sqns on his first tour during which he was awarded the DFC. Dispatched to Australia in 1943, he first served with 549 Sqn as a flight commander before joining 548. He served with the RAF after the war and later became chief production test pilot with Vickers Armstrong and then worked for British Aerospace. *(AHM of WA)*

Dave Glaser adopted this aircraft when he took command of the squadron. This aircraft is unique in having two opposing serial systems, RAF (JG655) and RAAF (A58-482), which was against all international regulations. However, who would ever complain knowing where it was based at the time! This Spitfire was also unique for its camouflage of Foliage Green and Dark Sea Grey over Sky Blue. Note also Glaser's personal emblem, a Musketeer, which was also present on his aircraft when he flew with 549 Sqn. JG655 was taken on charge by the RAF in March 1944 and arrived to Australia in June. It was scrapped in 1948.

were still with him when he saw Sgt Chandler collide with the other Spitfire which was actually flown by the CO himself. Neither of the two pilots involved in the collision survived and the squadron had lost its CO before becoming operational. As a temporary measure, F/L Watts took command.

Training continued in May without incident and at the end of the month the squadron began preparations to move to their new station, Livingstone, near Darwin. During the ferry flight on 10 June, led by two Beauforts for navigation purposes, the bad luck returned. After an hour and a half, while flying at 10,500 feet, P/O Davison's engine (A58-345) cut through some fault in the fuel system, and things became rather tense as the CO's R/T failed. The Beaufort went through the clouds to get a fix, closely followed by F/L Watts and F/L Calder who were closest. Davison eventually made a forced landing eight miles north of Proserpine. The others were too spread out to follow. The Beaufort provided a fix but P/O Davison was already heading for the coast and, as there was no V.H.F. in the Beaufort, nobody could tell him. F/O Cody gave a rendezvous to the rest of the formation and, as soon as E.T.A. was reached, the formation went down through the clouds only to find themselves out to sea under a low cloud base. Through some very good flying, excellent judgment, and perhaps a little change of luck, Magnetic Island was found and a safe landing executed. P/O Brown was most unfortunate and crashed after landing. Someone had left three oil drums in the middle of the runway!

The journey continued over the next few days and, on the 15th, on the last trip, it was P/O Griffiths' turn to encounter trouble when the engine of his Spitfire cut as he switched tanks (A58-359). He considered bailing but was too low to do so. Consequently, he fatally decided to make a forced landing in a forest. Even having arrived at their destination, the misfortune was not over for 548 as before the end of the month, during which training flights resumed, another Spitfire was lost when A58-376 encountered engine trouble on take-off and dived into the sea. The pilot, P/O Brown (the same involved in the 10 June accident), was severely injured and died of his two days later.

The squadron was declared fully operational on 4 July, but nothing happened that month except, once more, another crash that occurred on the 31st. In what was becoming all too common a cause of accidents, the engine of A58-394 failed on take-off. The Spitfire was badly damaged and was eventually written off. Fortunately, its pilot, F/Sgt Buchan, escaped major injury. In all, almost 370 hours were logged in July. The next day, 1 August, F/L R.A. Watts was officially given command of the unit and promoted to Squadron Leader. However, August proceeded just as July had. At readiness every day for seven days a week, by the end of month nothing had happened. That said, the squadron still logged over 450 hours. Compared to the previous months, however, September was seen as a busy month. On the 5th, 548 participated in its first offensive operation and, therefore, its first operational sorties. The target was a concealed campsite and enemy installations on Selaru Island. It was a series of low level

Squadron Leader Glaser leading six Spitfires of 548 Sqn in his personal mount (see previous page) for a photo shoot. Spitfire TS-P was A58-446.
(AHM of WA above and Andrew Thomas below)

Wearing the Squadron Leader pennant, Squadron Leader R.A. Watts' Spitfire A58-482/TS-M was photographed in October 1944 lined up with other Spitfires of the squadron. At that time, the unit's Spitfires had just been repainted in the standard RAAF Foliage Green camouflage. The last Spitfires, which had been issued to 548 in natural metal, were all repainted that month. *(Andrew Thomas)*

attacks in conjunction with the other Spitfire squadrons of No. 1 Fighter Wing. The squadron sent four aircraft - the CO in A58-482/TS-M, F/L J.A.C. Aiken in A58-353/TS-G, F/L L. Cheek in A58-320/W and W/O J.F. Isaac in A58-398/TS-Q. The operation was conducted without incident and the four Spitfires returned to base after three and half hours. On 17 September, two Spitfires scrambled to search for a small ship believed to be in difficulties but it seems it was being towed back to port when the two pilots (F/L K.V. Caldner in A58-334/TS-V and W/O M. Reid in A58-388/TS-U) found it. Two days later, two other pilots (W/O D.H. Shorland in A58-405/TS-D and W/O M. Reid A58-334/TS-V) scrambled but once more the aircraft intercepted, a Douglas transport, was found to be friendly. On 25 September, a bigger alert came to 548 at about 1710 when a section of A Flight was ordered to take-off to identify an aircraft. The pilots (F/L H.R. Palmer in A58-372/TS-J, F/L B.L. Price in A58-333/TS-C, F/Sgt R. Wichelo in A58-413/TS-L and F/Sgt R.I. Buchan in A58-395/TS-I) were vectored successfully to the aircraft which turned out to be another Douglas transport that was flying slightly off course to Darwin. The month ended without any further events and about 480 hours flown. This includes the activity of the detachment sent to Truscott.

Besides the move on the 22nd to Darwin's civilian aerodrome, October was uneventful despite over 400 hours being flown. November was worse with a little over 330 hours. In December, the Spitfires were grounded for defective glycol tubes. Repairs slowly progressed but, by the middle of the month, half a dozen of aircraft were serviceable. Despite this, the squadron was on readiness regularly but, generally speaking, December saw little aerial activity with only 62 hours flown. The year 1945 commenced as 1944 had ended with little activity and a mere 69 hours flown. On 9 February, the new CO arrived at the squadron to replace S/L Watts. Posted from 549 Squadron, S/L Ernest D. Glaser had been awarded the DFC while serving with 234 Squadron in 1942. His command became effective on the 14th. On the maintenance side, the glycol piping was still giving trouble and this hampered normal flying to the extent that only 65 hours were flown. The situation became better in March – 135 hours flown – but the lack of activity began to become a major issue and in April the number of hours logged did not exceed what had been done in March and an average of six Spitfires were available daily. On 20 May, while on detachment to Truscott, W/O Vassie had to belly-land during a night approach and his Spitfire caught fire in the process. Vassie received first-degree burns to several parts of his body but survived. Aerial activity rose to 260 hours that month.

In June, and for the first time in over eight months, 548 launched an offensive low-level attack on grounded aircraft in north-east Timor. Six aircraft participated in this operation led by the CO (A58-482/TS-V). The other pilots were F/L C.W.M. Saunders (A58-446/TS-P), F/L J.A.C. Aitken (A58-453/TS-A), F/L J.M. Hilton (A58-405/TS-D), F/L B.M. Price (A58-320/TS-W) and F/L F.S.R. Everill (A58-338/TS-X). All pilots returned home safely. Nevertheless, the personnel, especially the pilots, who had mostly

Three groundcrew posing in front of A58-482/TS-M. Note the two cannons in the wing, a rare installation in a Spitfire Mk. VIII. The two extra cannons were soon deleted and the aircraft returned as TS-V to become Glaser's aircraft. (AHM of WA)

been with the squadron for a year and a half, had the feeling that the only thing they did during that time was deteriorate their fighting and offensive spirit. Coupled with a low rate of serviceability, this was confirmed by the poor 180 hours logged for the month. This problem was also exacerbated by the lack of spares referred to previously while their best aircraft had been given to the other units in the Wing. In July, things didn't improve and the final fatal accident was recorded on the last day of the month when W/O Basil Clinton dived into the sea, while proceeding on a Navex, after an engine failure. His engine stopped at 5,000 feet and he was instructed by his section leader (F/L Aiken) to bail out which he tried to do at 1,500 feet when Clinton rolled the Spitfire on its back. He did not, however, appear to leave the Spitfire. The ASR mission returned to base without success. The next three months were equally uneventful except, at the end of August, the unit received Spitfire HF.VIIIs with which some flying was carried out. The squadron was disbanded on 9 October. In all, eighteen sorties were flown over almost two years. The squadron was the least active RAF fighter unit in terms of operations flown and time in existence.

Summary of the aircraft lost by accident - 548 Squadron

Date	Pilot	S/N	Origin	Serial	Code	Fate
19.04.44	S/L William H.A. **Wright**	RAF No. 70834	RAF	A58-393	TS-V	†
	Sgt Alan V. **Chandler**	RAF No. 1319672	RAF	A58-392	TS-G	†
10.06.44	P/O Allan E. **Davison**	RAF No. 160931	RAF	A58-345	TS-E	-
	P/O Norman C. **Brown**	RAF No. 159498	RAF	A58-383		-
15.06.44	P/O Frederick T. **Griffiths**	RAF No. 160936	RAF	A58-359	TS-V	†
29.06.44	P/O Norman C. **Brown** [1]	RAF No. 159498	RAF	A58-376		†
31.07.44	F/Sgt Robert I. **Buchan**	RAF No. 658955	RAF	A58-394	TS-G	-
20.05.45	W/O Henry J. **Vassie**	RAF No. 1361195	RAF	A58-399		-
31.07.45	W/O Basil **Clinton**	RAF No. 1615960	RAF	A58-372	TS-J	†

Total: 9

Above, the wreckage of A58-345/TS-E. It is surprising the pilot survived without major injury. A58-345 was previously JG346 and was taken on charge in October 1943.
Below, the result of an engine failure on take-off experienced by F/Sgt Buchan on 31 July 1944. The aircraft was not repaired. Taken on RAF charge in October 1943 as JG373, it reached Australia in February 1944. It was also the first Mk. VIII issued to 548.
(AHM of WA)

April 1944
September 1945

Victories - confirmed or probable claims: -

First operational sortie:
16.07.44
Last operational sortie:
31.07.45

Number of sorties: 30

Total aircraft written-off: 5

Aircraft lost on operations: -
Aircraft lost in accidents: 5

Squadron code letters:
ZF

COMMANDING OFFICERS				
S/L Eric P.W. Bocock	RAF No. 61215	RAF	15.12.43	09.10.45

SQUADRON USAGE

Also formed on 15 December as part of No.1 Fighter Wing, No. 549 Squadron was placed under the leadership of S/L E.P.W. Bocock, a former pilot of 72 and 602 Squadrons who had claimed five aircraft destroyed and two probables so far. He was, therefore, a very experienced pilot with a DFC ribbon on his chest. He was to be the squadron's only CO. He arrived several days after

This pilot can be easily identified by the Musketeer artwork painted on the fuselage. Dave Glaser poses here with two Australians fitters. Glaser was a flight commander at the time. Manned by British pilots, the three RAF squadrons of No. 1 Wing were serviced by RAAF groundcrew.
(Andrew Thomas)

Pilots of 549 Sqn pose for the photographer. They had plenty of time to do that!
Standing: F/L J.R. Williams, F/L W.B. Van N. Wedd, S/L E.P.W. Bocock (CO) and F/L J.F. Webster
Front row: W/O A.V. Franks, W/O J. Beaton and F/L G.L.V. Turner.

officially taking command on 1 January 1944. Like 548, the squadron moved to Strathpine on 19 January but took time to reach its full strength. For a while the squadron had nine pilots and no aircraft. The first Spitfires arrived on 7 April (A58-336 and A58-341) and by the end of the month A58-332, 335, 343, 347, 348, 373, 379, 381, 402 were on hand. The complement of aircraft was completed in May by which time the squadron had its full complement of pilots and machines. Unlike 548, the unit didn't encounter any major incidents during its training program and in mid-June the squadron moved to Strauss, in the Northern Territory, and sent a regular detachment to Truscott. On 16 July, the squadron was called for its first possible interception and four Spitfires led by F/L W.B. Webb (the other pilots were F/O R.R. Mills, F/O D. Fuller and W/O N. Thorpe) took off at 1650 only to return to base twenty minutes later having confirmed it was a friendly aircraft. As with 548, the lack of activity caused the pilots, from time to time, to find something to do, sometimes with fatal results. On 6 August, F/O K.J. Hadley was killed as a passenger on board a No. 2 Squadron Mitchell during an operational sortie. On 21 August, another scramble took place and eleven Spitfires became airborne, led by F/L Ernest D. Glaser DFC (one of the flight commanders and another experienced former 234 Squadron pilot), but, once more, the 'hostile' aircraft turned out to be friendly. In September, the squadron participated in a strafing mission on the 5th. Squadron Leader Bocock led a five aircraft formation to Selaru Island without incident. So far, the squadron had been lucky with no accidents to report, the complete opposite of 548. Its luck ran out from the end of October. It all started on the 28th when F/O Tickner blew a tyre on landing and ran off the strip to prevent the aircraft behind crashing into him. The incident ended without serious consequences for the pilot and aircraft (A58-332). Two days later, F/L 'Mike' Wedd undershot the strip, hit a drain and snapped off his starboard undercarriage leg. He bounced and landed about 200 yards down the strip and, when he hit the ground, the nose and port cannon dug into the tar causing the aircraft to spin around ending at right angles to the strip. Although the pilot escaped injury, the Spitfire, A58-335, was later declared as damaged beyond economical repair. It wasn't over as, one week later, F/O A.R.H. Palmer was killed while proceeding to Truscott. On the way over, Palmer reported that his oil pressure had dropped to zero. F/L Glaser, who was leading the formation, told him to bail out but instead of doing so he tried to ditch his aircraft in the sea

Liberator A72-67/GR-O being escorted by Spitfires of 549 Sqn over Northern Australia. Usually, this event occurred when the wing was called to identify a suspicious radar plot. *(AHM of WA)*

and was seen to go straight in. He was posted missing and even though a naval vessel was sent to search for him, he was not found. Bad times were to continue for the squadron which sadly lost another pilot and two aircraft on 16 November. Four pilots set out to take over the duty at Truscott. As they were preparing to land, W/O R. Possé and W/O L.C. Bushell collided in mid-air. Possé crashed and was killed but W/O Bushell managed to bail out successfully although slightly injured. The run of bad luck ended five days later when F/O J.P. Maguire was obliged to make a forced landing at Darwin's civilian aerodrome and suffered a broken collarbone and other minor injuries. The Spitfire was only good for scrapping. November was the worst month since the formation of the squadron but none of this overshadowed the longest Spitfire raid of the war on the 27th. The orders were to strafe and destroy the two enemy radar facilities near Cape Lore on the south-east coast of Timor. The attack formation was made up of four No. 2 Squadron Mitchells, ten Spitfires from 549 (led by the CO) and two flown by No. 1 Wing staff - G/C B.R. Walker and W/C R.C. Wilkinson. The Spitfires were to strafe the installations first and then the Mitchells were to bomb and strafe what was left. The fighters refueled at Austin en route but only seven aircraft were able to get airborne as the others experienced air locks in their fuel systems. The operation, widely reported in the press, involved a round trip of nearly 800 miles, a record for the Spitfire. Whatever the results obtained, considered good at the time, the operation provided a much needed morale boost at a time when morale across the Wing was very low. After that, the war was effectively over for the squadron if we excuse the participation of S/L Bocock in an operation on 3 June in A58-438. He was acting as Wing Commander for a raid on Cape Chester strip on the northern end of Timor. Two scrambles in July, one on the 26th, and one on the 31st, were carried out by F/O R. Lane and, of course, were uneventful. These were the final operational sorties. The last Spitfires left the squadron on 24 September and 549 was disbanded on 9 October.

Summary of the aircraft lost by accident - 549 Squadron

Date	Pilot	S/N	Origin	Serial	Code	Fate
30.10.44	F/L William B. vN. **Wedd**	RAF No. 76972	RAF	**A58-335**	ZF-D	-
08.11.44	F/O Alfred R.H. **Palmer**	RAF No. 130639	RAF	**A58-347**	ZF-F	†
16.11.44	W/O Ronald W. **Possé**	RAF No. 1377971	RAF	**A58-300**	ZF-M	†
	W/O Leslie C. **Bushell**	RAF No. 1314286	RAF	**A58-364**	ZF-L	-
21.11.44	P/O James P. **Maguire**	RAF No. 158914	RAF	**A58-403**	ZF-K	-

Total: 5

Above, A58-335/ZF-D after its crash of 30 October 1944 and, below, A58-403/ZD-K which crashed on 21 November. *(AHM of WA)*

The A58 Register (simplified)

Only operational units and OTUs are shown in this register. It is based on the movement cards which means that some physical movements might have never taken place.

300: 54, 549 *(ZF-M)*
301: 452, 54 *(DL-A, then DL-K)*, 549
302: 54, 452, 54
303: -
304: 452, 54, 549 *(ZF-K)*
305: 452
306: 548, 54
307: 452, 457, 54, 548
308: 452, 549
309: 452, 54
310: 452, 54, 452, 54
311: 452, 54 *(DL-P)*, 452, 54
312: 452, 54
313: 452
314: 452 *(QY-F)*, 54, 452
315: -
316: 452, 54
317: 54 *(DL-Y)*, 548
318: 452, 54 *(DL-F)*, 452, 54
319: 548
320: 548 *(TS-W)*
321: 54, 549
322: 549 *(ZF-L)*
323: 54, 549 *(ZF-B)*
324: -
325: 548
326: 549 *(ZF-T)*
327: 54 *(DL-J)*
328: 457, 54, 549
329: 54
330: 452, 54 *(DL-C)*
331: 452, 54 *(DL-L)*, 452, 54
332: 549 *(ZF-L)*
333: 548 *(TS-C)*
334: 548 *(TS-V)*
335: 549 *(ZF-D)*
336: 549
337: 549
338: 548 *(TS-X)*, 54
339: 452, 54
340: 452
341: 549 *(ZF-A)*
342: 452
343: 549
344: 452
345: 548 *(TS-E)*
346: -
347: 549 *(ZF-F)*
348: 549 *(ZF-S)*
349: 54 *(DL-O)*
350: 548
351: 549 *(ZF-H)*
352: 54 *(DL-N)*, 548
353: 548 *(TS-G)*, 54
354: 54
355: 54 *(DL-Z)*, 548
356: 457 *(ZP-K)*, 54 *(DL-U)*
357: 54 *(DL-R)*
358: 457, 549
359: 548
360: 452, 54 *(DL-R)*
361: 452, 549
362: 54 *(DL-X)*
363: 549 *(ZF-B)*
364: 549 *(ZF-M)*
365: 549
366: 457 *(ZP-G)*
367: -
368: -
369: 452, 54 *(DL-F)*
370: 54
371: 54
372: 548 *(TS-J)*
373: 549 *(ZF-W)*
374: 548
375: 452, 54
376: 548
377: 452
378: 548
379: 549
380: 54
381: 549 *(ZF-Z)*
382: 452, 54, 548 *(TS-M)*
383: 548
384: 54
385: 457 *(ZP-O)*
386: 54
387: 452
388: 548 *(TS-U)*
389: 452
390: 54 *(DL-M)*
391: 54 *(DL-Z)*
392: 548 *(TS-G)*
393: 548 *(TS-V)*
394: 548 *(TS-G)*
395: 548 *(TS-I)*

Left, A58-317/DL-V, one of the rare 54 Sqn Spitfire VIIIs with a white tail. Below, A58-327 of 54 Sqn after its landing accident of 5 March 1945. The aircraft was repaired and returned to service. It was struck off in November 1948.
(AHM of WA)

Left, A58-356/DL-U of 54 Sqn on its back after the accident that put an end to its career with the RAAF in April 1945.
(AHM of WA)

Spitfire A58-379 ZF-Z, wearing Flight Lieutenant Glaser's personal Musketeer marking, seen at Darwin in 1944. *(Andrew Thomas)*

396: 548
397: 548, 54
398: 548 *(TS-Q)*
399: 548
400: 457 *(ZP-M)*, 452
401: 452
402: 549 *(ZF-C)*
403: 549 *(ZF-K)*
404: 549
405: 548, 54
406: 549 *(ZF-R)*
407: 452
408: 54 *(DL-T)*
409: 548
410: 452, 457
411: 452 *(QY-P)*
412: 548
413: 548 *(TS-L)*
414: 549
415: 549
416: 549
417: 452
418: 457 *(ZP-Y)*, 549
419: 457 *(ZP-Y)*, 452
420: 452 *(QY-Y)*
421: 549
422: 548
423: -
424: -
425: -
426: -
427: 452 *(QY-Q later QY-X)*
428: 457, 54 *(DL-B)*
429: 452, 54
430: 452 *(ZP-Y)*
431: 548 *(V)*
432: 54, 548
433: 452, 457 *(CR-C)*
434: 79
435: 452
436: 452, 79
437: 54
438: 549 *(ZF-V)*
439: 54
440: 452
441: -
442: 8 OTU
443: -
444: -
445: -
446: 548 *(TS-P)*, 54

449: -
450: 457, 452
451: 548, 54
452: -
453: 548 *(TS-A)*
454: 548, 54, 548
455: -
456: 452
457: 457 *(ZP-Z)*
458: 457, 452
459: 457
460: 457, 54
461: 457, 548 *(TS-P)*
462: 54
463: 457
464: 457, 8 OTU
465: 457 *(ZP-H)*, 452
466: 457, 452
467: 457 *(ZP-S)*
468: -
469: 457, 54
470: 457, 54
471: 457
472: -
473: -
474: 54 *(DL-J)*
475: 457
476: 54 *(DL-W)*
477: 457, 452 *(QY-X)*
478: 457, 452
479: 54 *(DL-H)*
480: 54 *(DL-Y)*
481: -
482: 548 *(TS-M)*
483: 549
484: 457 *(CR-C)*, 452
485: -
486: 8 OTU
487: 79 *(UP-S)*
488: -
489: 79 *(UP-L)*
490: 452, 79
491: -
492: 79 *(UP-B and UP-U)*
493: -
494: 54
495: 79 *(UP-J)*
496: 452 *(QY-M)*
497: 457 *(RG-V)*
498: 54 *(DL-D)*
499: -

Three Spitfires of 54 Sqn. Top, A58-360/DL-R and, above, A58-480/DL-Y with the serial painted in black. It was painted in light grey on DL-R.
Left, the wreckage of A58-474/DL-E after its accident. The pilot, F/O F.F. Thomas was lucky to survive the crash but his luck ran out as he was killed two months later in another crash.
(AHM of WA)

500: 54, 452 *(QY-D)*
501: 79 *(UP-H)*
502: 452
503: 452
504: 452 *(QY-E later QY-R)*
505: 79 *(UP-D later UP-S)*
506: 79 *(UP-U)*
507: 79
508: 79 *(UP-E)*
509: 79
510: 452
511: 79
512: 79 *(UP-Y)*
513: 79 *(UP-X)*
514: 79
515: 457 *(ZP-Q)*
516: 452 *(QY-T)*
517: 79 *(UP-F)*
518: 452 *(CR-C)*
519: 452
520: 452
521: 452 *(QY-S)*
522: 79 *(UP-A)*
523: 5 OTU, 8 OTU
524: 452 *(QY-C)*
525: 452
526: 79 *(UP-R)*
527: 79
528: 457, 452
529: -

530: -
531: 79 *(UP-C)*
532: 452
533: 452
534: 452 *(QY-R)*
535: 5 OTU
536: 5 OTU, 8 OTU
537: 452
538: 5 OTU, 8 OTU
539: 79 *(UP-M)*
540: 452
541: -
542: -
543: 79 *(UP-? later UP-N)*
544: 79
545: 79
546: 79
547: 79 *(UP-O)*
548: -
549: -
550: -
551 to 599 not allocated
600: 457 *(ZP-X)*
601: -
602: 457 *(RG-V)*, 452
603: -
604: 457 *(ZP-D)*
605: 457
606: 457 *(ZP-W)*
607: 457

The first two Spitfire HF.VIIIs arrived in September 1944 and A58-601 was the first to be assembled. It was never issued to any operational squadron but was used at No. 1 Aircraft Performance Unit for type performance trials. At that time, the white empennage and leading edges have been added. Note that A58-600 was originally assigned serial A58-551, continuing the sequence, but in October the RAAF decided to start a new sequence for the type.

608: -
609: 457 *(ZP-S)*
610: 457
611: 457 *(ZP-B)*
612: -
613: 457
614: 457
615: 457 *(ZP-Y)*
616: 457
617: 457, 79
618: 457
619: 452 *(QY-G)*
620: 457
621: 457
622: 457
623: 457
624: 457, 54, 548
625: -
626: 457
627: 457 *(ZP-Z)*
628: -
629: 457
630: 457
631: 457 *(ZP-V)*
632: -
633: 457
634: 452, 457
635: 457 *(ZP-R)*
636: 452
637: -
638: 79
639: 79, 457 *(ZP-V)*
640: 79 *(UP-W)*
641: 452
642: 457
643: 79 *(UP-K)*
644: -
645: 79 *(UP-V)*
646: 452 *(QY-Y)*
647: 452 *(QY-V)*
648: 457
649: 457
650: 452
651: 79 *(UP-Z)*
652: 457
653: 452
654: 79 *(UP-H)*
655: -
656: -
657: -
658: -
659: -
660: -
661: -
662: -
663: -
664: -
665: -
666: -
667: -
668: -
669: -
670: -
671: -
672: 457 *(ZP-Y)*
673: -
674: -
675: -
676: -
677: -
678: -
679: -
680: -
681: -
682: -
683: -
684: -
685: -
686: -
687: -
688: -
689: 79
690: -
691: -
692: -
693: -
694: -
695: -
696: -
697: -
698: -
699: -
700: -
701: -
702: -
703: -
704: -
705: -
706: -
707: -
708: -
709: -

710: -	**735:** -
711: -	**736:** -
712: -	**737:** -
713: -	**738:** -
714: -	**739:** -
715: -	**740:** -
716: -	**741:** -
717: -	**742:** -
718: -	**743:** -
719: -	**744:** -
720: 452 *(QY-O)*	**745:** -
721: -	**746:** -
722: -	**747:** -
723: -	**748:** -
724: -	**749:** -
725: -	**750:** -
726: -	**751:** -
727: -	**752:** -
728: -	**753:** -
729: -	**754:** -
730: -	**755:** -
731: -	**756:** -
732: 79	**757:** -
733: -	**758:** -
734: -	

About one third of the Spitfire VIIIs sent to Australia were never issued to any units and were stored before being scrapped after the war with just a couple of hours on their airframes. The RAAF did not save any for preservation. *(AHM of WA)*

IN MEMORIAM

Spitfire Mk. VIII
(SWPac British squadrons)

Name	Service No	Rank	Age	Origin	Date	Serial
Brown, Norman Colenso	RAF No. 159498	F/O	21	RAF	01.07.44	A58-376
Brown, Peter George Fleming	RAF No. 120926	F/L	22	RAF	19.04.44	A58-309
Chandler, Alan Victor	RAF No. 1319672	F/Sgt	22	RAF	19.04.44	A58-392
Clinton, Basil	RAF No. 198796	P/O	22	RAF	31.07.45	A58-372
Fox, Peter	RAF No. 188187	P/O	n/k	RAF	05.10.44	A58-310
Griffiths, Frederick Thomas	RAF No. 160936	F/O	21	RAF	15.06.44	A58-359
Meakin, Frederick	RAF No. 123140	F/L	23	RAF	28.07.44	A58-390
Palmer, Alfred Richard Harry	RAF No. 130639	F/L	21	RAF	08.11.44	A58-347
Possé, Ronald Walter	RAF No. 1377971	W/O	22	RAF	16.11.44	A58-300
Thomas, Fredereick Francis	RAF No. 155264	F/O	22	RAF	17.06.45	A58-309
Wright, William Henry Alexander	RAF No. 70834	S/L	26	RAF	19.04.44	A58-393

Total: 11
United Kingdom: 11

Squadron Leader Dave Glaser banking in his Spitfire in April 1945.

Supermarine Spitfire LF.VIII A58-317 (ex-JF936)
No. 54 Squadron
Livingstone (NT, Australia), summer 1944

Supermarine Spitfire LF.VIII A58-370 (ex-JG603)
No. 54 Squadron
Darwin Civil (NT, Australia), spring 1945

Supermarine Spitfire LF.VIII A58-360 (ex-JG376)
No. 54 Squadron
Darwin Civil (NT, Australia), spring 1945

Supermarine Spitfire LF.VIII A58-482 (ex-JG655)
No. 548 Squadron
Squadron Leader Ernest D. GLASER
Darwin (NT, Australia), summer 1945

Supermarine Spitfire LF.VIII A58-482 (ex-JG655)
No. 548 Squadron
Squadron Leader Raymond A. WATTS
Darwin (NT, Australia), October 1944

Supermarine Spitfire LF.VIII A58-379 (ex-JG270)
No. 549 Squadron
Flight Lieutenant Ernest D. GLASER
Darwin Civil (NT, Australia), autumn 1944

Supermarine Spitfire LF.VIII A58-322 (ex-JF942)
No. 549 Squadron
Darwin Civil (NT, Australia), autumn 1944

SQUADRONS! - The series

1. The Supermarine Spitfire Mk VI
2. The Republic Thunderbolt Mk I
3. The Supermarine Spitfire Mk V in the Far East
4. The Boeing Fortress Mk I
5. The Supermarine Spitfire Mk XII
6. The Supermarine Spitfire Mk VII
7. The Supermarine Spitfire F. 21
8. The Handley Page Halifax Mk I
9. The Forgotten Fighters
10. The NA Mustang IV in Western Europe
11. The NA Mustang IV over the Balkans and Italy
12. The Supermarine Spitfire Mk XVI - *The British*
13. The Martin Marauder Mk I
14. The Supermarine Spitfire Mk VIII in the Southwest Pacific - *The British*
15. The Gloster Meteor F.I & F.III
16. The NA Mitchell - *The Dutch, Poles and French*
17. The Curtiss Mohawk
18. The Curtiss Kittyhawk Mk II
19. The Boulton Paul Defiant - *day and night fighter*
20. The Supermarine Spitfire Mk VIII in the Southwest Pacific - *The Australians*
21. The Boeing Fortress Mk II & Mk III
22. The Douglas Boston and Havoc - *The Australians*
23. The Republic Thunderbolt Mk II
24. The Douglas Boston and Havoc - *Night fighters*
25. The Supermarine Spitfire Mk V - *The Eagles*
26. The Hawker Hurricane - *The Canadians*
27. The Supermarine Spitfire Mk V - *The 'Bombay' squadrons*
28. The Consolidated Liberator - *The Australians*
29. The Supermarine Spitfire Mk XVI - *The Dominions*
30. The Supermarine Spitfire Mk V - *The Belgian and Dutch squadrons*
31. The Supermarine Spitfire Mk V - *The New-Zealanders*
32. The Supermarine Spitfire Mk V - *The Norwegians*
33. The Brewster Buffalo
34. The Supermarine Spitfire Mk II - *The Foreign squadrons*
35. The Martin Marauder Mk II
36. The Supermarine Spitfire Mk V - *The Special Reserve squadrons*
37. The Supermarine Spitfire Mk XIV - *The Belgian and Dutch squadrons*
38. The Supermarine Spitfire Mk II - *The Rhodesian, Dominion & Eagle squadrons*
39. The Douglas Boston and Havoc - *Intruders*
40. The North American Mustang Mk III over Italy and the Balkans (Pt-1)
41. The Bristol Brigand
42. The Supermarine Spitfire Mk V - *The Australians*
43. The Hawker Typhoon - *The Rhodesian squadrons*
44. The Supermarine Spitfire F.22 & F.24
45. The Supermarine Spitfire Mk IX - *The Belgian and Dutch squadrons*
46. The North American & CAC Mustang - *The RAAF*
47. The Westland Whirlwind
48. The Supermarine Spitfire Mk XIV - *The British squadrons*
49. The Supermarine Spitfire Mk I - *The beginning (the Auxiliary squadrons)*
50. The Hawker Tempest Mk V - *The New Zealanders*
51. The Last of the Long-Range Biplane Flying Boats
52. The Supermarine Spitfire Mk IX - *The Former Canadian Homefront squadrons*
53. The Hawker Hurricane Mk I & Mk II - *The Eagle squadrons*
54. The Hawker biplane fighters
55. The Supermarine Spitfire Mk IX - *The Auxiliary squadrons*
56. The Hawker Typhoon - *The Canadian squadrons*
57. The Douglas SBD - *New Zealand and France*
58. The Forgotten Patrol Seaplanes
59. The Dutch Fighter Squadrons - *Nos. 322 & 120 (NEI) Squadrons*
60. The Supermarine Spitfire - *The Australian Squadrons in Western Europe and the Med*
61. The Belgian Fighter Squadrons - *Nos. 349 & 350 Squadrons*
62. The Supermarine Spitfire Mk I - *The beginning (the Regular squadrons)*
63. The Hawker Typhoon - *The 'Fellowship of the Bellows' squadrons*
64. The North American Mustang Mk I & Mk II
65. The Eagle Squadrons *Nos. 71, 121 & 133 Squadrons*
66. The Handley Page Hampden *Torpedo-bomber*
67. The North American Mustang Mk III over Italy and the Balkans (Pt-2)

Introducing's RAF In Combat and Bravo Bravo Aviation's collection of highly-detailed and historically accurate, high-quality aviation prints. For more information on available prints, please visit:

 or

Prints in connection with the book:

PL-202: S. Linnard
PL-213: E.P.W. Bocock

www.ingramcontent.com/pod-product-compliance
Lightning Source LLC
Chambersburg PA
CBHW060823090426
42738CB00002B/85